The Contemporary Condition book series offers a sustained inquiry into the contemporary condition from a range of perspectives by key commentators who investigate contemporaneity as a defining condition of our historical present. Contemporaneity refers to the temporal complexity that follows from the coming together in the same cultural space of heterogeneous clusters generated along different historical trajectories, across different scales, and in different localities. With the overall aim of questioning the formation of subjectivity in time and the concept of temporality in the world now, it is a basic assumption that art can operate as an advanced laboratory for investigating processes of meaning-making and for understanding wider developments within culture and society. The series identifies three broad lines of inquiry for investigation: the issue of temporality, the role of contemporary media and computational technologies, and how artistic practice makes epistemic claims.

Sternberg Press

THE CONTEMPORARY CONDITION

THE CONTEMPORARY CONDITION 01

The Contemporary Condition:
Introductory Thoughts on Contemporaneity and Contemporary Art
Geoff Cox & Jacob Lund

Published by Sternberg Press, 2016

Series edited by Geoff Cox & Jacob Lund

Published in partnership with ARoS Aarhus Art Museum
and The Contemporary Condition research project
at Aarhus University, made possible by a grant
from the Danish Council for Independent Research,
September 2015 – August 2018.

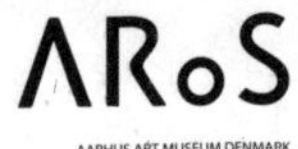

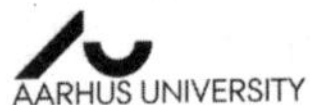

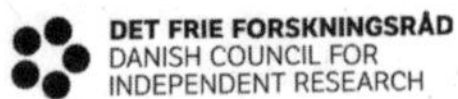

contemporaneity.au.dk

Special thanks to Anne Kølbæk Iversen and Verina Gfader
for editorial and production support.

Design: Dexter Sinister
Printing and binding: BUD Potsdam
Paper: Cyclus Offset

ISBN 978-3-95679-281-6

Sternberg Press
Caroline Schneider
Karl-Marx-Allee 78
D-10243 Berlin
www.sternberg-press.com

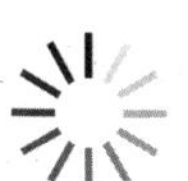

The Contemporary Condition: Introductory Thoughts on Contemporaneity & Contemporary Art

Geoff Cox & Jacob Lund

What do we mean when we say that something is contemporary? And what does—or perhaps *should*—the designator "contemporary art" refer to? An immediate response would be that contemporary art is an art of the present, that it somehow addresses and expresses the present. But what is this present; what is our, or more objectively, *the* present? What constitutes the *present* present or the *contemporary* contemporary? When did it begin? And how far does it extend spatially? When and where does it end, and why do these questions matter?

Our present is a present, we claim, characterized by contemporaneity in the sense that it is a present constituted by the bringing together of a multitude of different temporalities on different scales, including different grand narratives and imagined communities of nation-states and cultural clusters developed during modernity. Our present is formed by an intensified global interconnectedness of different times and experiences of time that both challenge as well as consolidate some of the hierarchies that have been associated with modernity. Thus, the contemporary is at once a periodizing category in the sense that it is our era, the time in which we live, and a modal or experiential category in the sense that it is a particular relationship to time and to history, or maybe an experience of a loss of history, of a loss of a futural moment.

The basic human experience of the temporal has, at least since Martin Heidegger, been understood in terms of an original *ek-stasis*, a dislocation or dispersion, which transgresses the interiority of the subject and connects it to its surroundings and other subjects, living and passed away. Interiority and exteriority are thus two sides of an original temporalizing movement, a "primordial outside of itself."[1] Human existence

1. Martin Heidegger, *Sein und Zeit* (Tübingen: Niemeyer, 1927/86), 329. In English translation by J. Stambaugh as *Being and Time* (Albany: SUNY Press, 2010), with original pagination in the margin. We here draw upon Hans Ruin, "Time as Ek-stasis and Trace of the Other," in *Rethinking Time: Essays on History, Memory, and Representation*, ed. Hans Ruin and Andrus Ers (Stockholm: Södertörn Philosophical Studies 10, 2011), 51–62.

does not take place *in* time, it is rather through our existence that we "temporalize" [*zeitigen*], opening ourselves up towards the future, which constantly comes into being as an anticipation of a not-yet: "Having-been arises from the future, in such a way that the future that has-been (or better 'is in the process of having been') releases the present from itself. This unified phenomenon of the future that makes present in the process of having-been is what we call temporality."[2] Roughly put, we thus ek-statically form ourselves by projecting ourselves into a future and the present becomes present through this projective transcending and self-transcending movement. We experience the present via the anticipation of the primary phenomenon of time that is the future, that is, via something that is not present yet and renders the present something that will have been. Without going deeper into the existential-ontological register of Heidegger we would like to connect this insight to broader reflections on current possibilities for social and political change in a time when it seems that the phenomenon of the future is being extinguished (or usurped by predictive algorithms), when collective ekstacy and protention have been rendered seemingly impossible.

* * *

With accelerated globalization, the concomitant ubiquitous influence of information technologies and spread of neoliberalism over the last three decades, after the so-called "end of history," disparate cultures and art worlds have become interconnected and con-temporaneous with each other, forming

2. Heidegger, *Sein und Zeit*, 326.

3. This point is noted by a number of art historians, sociologists, cultural critics, and scholars from a number of other disciplines, among them Terry Smith, Alexander Alberro, Nikos Papastergiadis, and Marc Augé. See, for instance, Terry Smith, Okwui Enwezor and Nancy Condee, eds., *Antinomies of Art and Culture: Modernity, Postmodernity, Contemporaneity* (Durham: Duke University Press, 2008); Terry Smith, "Contemporary Art and Contemporaneity," *Critical Inquiry* 32 (Summer 2006): 681–707; Terry Smith, *Contemporary Art: World Currents* (London: Laurence King Publishing, 2011); Nikos Papastergiadis

global networks of influence.[3] During this period, we have also gradually replaced the term "modern art," and for a period "postmodern art," with "contemporary art" as descriptor of the art of our historical present. This can be detected in the fact that a large number of art museums and newly established international biennials define themselves as institutional agents of "contemporary art" rather than "modern art." This shift from modernity to an era of contemporaneity is connected to the realization that time changes with the events that fill it, and that time itself has a history and politics. Time is constructed and reconstructed, multiple, and asymmetrical. As Walter Benjamin remarks in his fourteenth thesis on the philosophy of history: "History is the subject of a structure whose site is not homogenous, empty time, but time filled by the presence of the now [*Jetztzeit*]."[4] As well as Benjamin's use of the term "Jetztzeit" indicates something more complex than simply *Gegenwart* [now, presence, or the present], the term "contemporaneity" should not be understood merely as a periodizing category nor "the contemporary" as the historical style of such a period. Rather it operates as a designator of the changing temporal quality of the historical present, which is not—as we will try to explain based in particular on the analyses by philosopher Peter Osborne and art historian and theorist Terry Smith—simply a coming together *in* time, but *of* times.[5]

and Victoria Lynn, eds., *Art in the Global Present* (Sydney: UTS ePress, 2014); accessed August 22, 2016, http://epress.lib.uts.edu.au/books/art-global-present; Nikos Papastergiadis, *Cosmopolitanism and Culture* (Cambridge: Polity, 2012); Marc Augé, *Pour une anthropologie des mondes contemporains* (Paris: Aubier, 1994); and Alexander Alberro, "Periodising Contemporary Art," in *Theory in Contemporary Art Since 1985*, ed. Zoya Kocur and Simon Leung (Malden, MA: Wiley-Blackwell, 2012), 64–71.

4. Walter Benjamin, "On the Concept of History," in *Selected Writings, vol. 4, 1938–1940*, eds. Eiland and Jennings (Cambridge, MA: Belknap Press, 1992), 395.

5. On "a temporal unity in disjunction, or a disjunctive unity of present times," see Peter Osborne, *Anywhere or Not at All: Philosophy of Contemporary Art* (London: Verso, 2013), 17. On temporal complexity, history, and anachronism in works of art, see also Georges Didi-Huberman, *L'Œil de l'histoire* I–IV (Paris: Éditions Minuit, 2009–12) and Giorgio Agamben, "What is the Contemporary?," [2008], in *What is an Apparatus? And Other Essays*, trans. David Kishik and Stefan Pedatella (Stanford: Stanford University Press, 2009), 39–54.

In general the totalizing logic of periodization now more than ever seems over-determined, insofar as the unity that such logic claims to establish is undermined by a number of different special histories and coexisting mixed temporalities that constantly resist assimilation.[6] Thus, it should be stressed that the coming together of temporalities is necessarily uneven and layered, and that the "era of contemporaneity" has come into being without any clean breaks or paradigmatic ruptures. This is not to say that totalizing logics of temporalization are to be abstained from altogether. Indeed grasping such logics is in a certain sense a prerequisite for political action. At the level of social organization to temporalize is to inscribe subjects within a historical form and temporalization thus determines the actions that are possible within this structure.[7] Required, therefore, is more critical reflection on periodizing logic in itself as temporal form in order to more fully understand the conceptual logic that underpins the way we identify periods, movements, styles, and techniques as forms of time more broadly.[8] In a similar way we might begin to understand other periodizing categorizations such as Arthur Danto's older notion of "post-historical art" or the currently fashionable notion of "post-internet art" as demonstrations of the onto-epistemological confusions that are now operative in aesthetic production.[9] Moreover we might

6. See Harry Harootunian, "Remembering the Historical Present," *Critical Inquiry*, vol. 33, no. 3 (Spring 2007): 471–494.

7. See Peter Osborne, "Temporalization as Transcendental Aesthetics: Avant-Garde, Modern, Contemporary," in *The Nordic Journal of Aesthetics*, no. 44–45 (2012–13): 28–49.

8. Indeed this is what Osborne has called for in his discussion of the temporalities of modern, postmodern and contemporary periodizations. To Osborne temporalization is a practice of transcendental aesthetics and as such it is the process of the production of subjects. See Peter Osborne, "Temporalization as Transcendental Aesthetics: Avant-Garde, Modern, Contemporary."

9. We see such confusions addressed directly in Hito Steyerl's essay "Too Much World: Is the Internet Dead?," *e-flux journal*, no. 49 (2013), accessed August 24, 2016, http://www.e-flux.com/journal/too-much-world-is-the-internet-dead/, where she claims that reality itself is post-produced, and certain artworks like those of Oliver Laric who questions the past and the present states of objects, accessed September 1, 2016, http://oliverlaric.com/.

argue that more critical attention to the temporality expressed through such concepts might usefully reveal the cultural logic of their reification or underlying political function.[10]

It should be clear by now that one of our main claims is that the contemporary version of contemporary differs from the contemporary of previous decades. Something has happened in our relation to time, how we exist in time, and the ways in which our conception of time relates to our conception of art. We consider art to be a particularly important cultural carrier of contemporaneity inasmuch as it has increasingly created transnational spaces in which contemporaneity is thematized, represented (sometimes even produced) and made an object of experience. As Osborne has observed, contemporary art biennials in particular appear as cultural spaces where similarities and differences between geopolitically diverse forms of social experience are being represented and explored within the parameters of a common world.[11] As such our interest is therefore in contemporary art forms that in different ways are concerned with the issue of temporality and constitution of subjectivity in our historical present. Fundamentally this is what makes them worthy of the predicate "contemporary," we argue.

The distinctiveness of contemporaneity is the way it refers to the temporal complexity that follows from the coming together in the same cultural space of heterogeneous cultural clusters generated along different historical trajectories, across different scales, and in different localities. This matters inasmuch as it draws into question the formation of subjectivity in time and the concept of temporality in the world now.

10. See Geoff Cox, "Postscript on the Post-Digital and the Problem of Temporality," *Postdigital Aesthetics: Art, Computation and Design*, ed. David M. Berry and Michael Dieter (Basingstoke: Palgrave Macmillan, 2015), 151–162.

11. See Peter Osborne, *Anywhere or Not at All: Philosophy of Contemporary Art*, 27. For a critique of the biennial as a systemic form that articulates the temporal logic of capital accumulation, see Peter Osborne, "Existential Urgency: Contemporaneity, Biennials and Social Form," *The Nordic Journal of Aesthetics*, no. 49–50 (2015): 175–188.

If postcolonial temporality appeared as a multiplicity of times existing together,[12] it is becoming more and more evident that the plurality of times today are not only existing at the same time, in parallel to each other, but that they interconnect and are being brought to bear on the same present, a kind of planetary present even though of course it is unevenly distributed and shared. As has been remarked by historian and philosopher Achille Mbembe the plurality of times is "not a series but an *interlocking* of presents, pasts and futures that retain their depths of other presents, pasts and futures, each age bearing, altering and maintaining the previous ones."[13]

In this essay we aim to set out the discussion of what it means to assume contemporaneity to be a defining condition of our experience of time today. We consider this to be speculative in tone but no less urgent in beginning to uncover some of the complexities and interconnections of forces that shape our experience of time and our ability to act in the world—both politically and artistically. In a somewhat inconsecutive manner, which reflects the complexity of our object, we are trying to come to terms with the changes in how we understand the historical present in order to conceive of it "less badly,"[14] and to come to terms with the crisis of historical agency, the felt suspension of a futural moment and our inability to conceive of another world. Indeed we wish to explore the possibilities for reinstalling a social imagination beyond capitalism on these conditions, which to a large extent are the consequence of the development of that very capitalism without being reducible to it.

12. See Dipesh Chakrabarty, *Provincializing Europe: Postcolonial Thought and Historical Difference* (Princeton NJ: Princeton University Press, 2000), 109.

13. Achille Mbembe, *On the Postcolony* (Berkeley: University of California Press, 2001), 16.

14. We refer to Peter Osborne's phrase "Contemporary Art is badly known," which appears on the opening page of his *Anywhere or Not at All: Philosophy of Contemporary Art*. See also Geoff Cox and Jacob Lund, "Contemporary Conditions are Badly Known," *Acoustic Space*, vol. 16, (Center for New Media Culture RIXC in collaboration with Art Research Laboratory of Liepaja University, Riga, forthcoming 2017).

* * *

There are now many different co-existing ways of being in time and belonging to it. As Smith remarks when trying to localize the main currents within contemporary art:

> Many artists working today imagine the physical conjunction of a number of different kinds of world: the intimate, personal sense of "my world"; the close neighborhood of the local; nearby worlds, then increasingly distant beyonds, until a sense of the World in general is reached. In between these, and transversing them, are transitory spaces, "no-places," passages of physical trafficking and virtual interconnection. This multi-scalar picture also evokes both the geophysical adjacency of these worlds and their cultural co-temporality. It recognizes the differential rates of their movement through actual time, and the mobility of those whose lives weave between and through them.[15]

Thus, while being increasingly aware of being in the present, of the omnipresence of the present,[16] we are becoming attentive to other kinds of time and how these are

15. Terry Smith, "Contemporary Art: World Currents in Transition Beyond Globalization," in *The Global Contemporary: The Rise of New Art Worlds after 1989*, eds. Hans Belting, Andrea Buddensieg, Peter Weibel (Cambridge, MA: MIT Press for ZKM, Karlsruhe, 2013), 190.

16. On the omnipresence of the present and "presentism" as a time-relation that has no temporal horizon other than itself, see François Hartog, *Régimes d'historicité: Présentisme et expériences du temps* (Paris: Seuil, 2003), who argues for a new regime of historicity, which, in contrast to the modern regime of historicity, is focused on the present rather than the future. On the role of the category of the future in Modernity, see Reinhart Koselleck, *Vergangene Zukunft: Zur Semantik geschichtlicher Zeiten* (Frankfurt am Main: Suhrkamp, 1979) and Pierre Nora, "L'avènement mondial de la mèmoire," *Transit* no. 22 (2002), 18–31, accessed August 24, 2016, http://www.eurozine.com/articles/article_2002-04-19-nora-fr.html. We intend to unfold the discussion of the relationship between modernity, contemporaneity, and history in another publication in The Contemporary Condition book series.

interconnected. As a consequence, we seem to be living in an expanded present, a present in which several temporalities and times take part in what is perceived as present and as presence. This global contemporaneity means that networked informational technologies and ever more socialized media forms play a decisive role both in shaping the field of art and culture and in the ways in which art and culture themselves function and create meaning.[17] The Internet in particular has produced an extreme spatial and temporal compression marked by a perpetual sense of dislocation that gives rise to new forms of experience and "pseudo-presence."[18] This—as the editors of *e-flux journal* acknowledge in their introduction to the issue "The End of the End of History?"—alters the ways in which we remember and experience places, events and time itself as everything appears to be happening as if contemporaneously.[19] It becomes increasingly evident that our being is a networked and connective being, and that if "every culture is first and foremost a particular experience of time," as Giorgio Agamben insists[20]—or if every culture is first and foremost a particular experience of what takes actively part in the constitution of the present, we might say—then concepts of identity, subjectivity and community require urgent renegotiation. How does art relate to such a condition? It is, we claim, a main task for contemporary artistic practices to investigate this condition and additionally to negotiate the significant role of media and information technologies in the interconnection of times and life worlds.

17. Bruno Latour's actor-network theory is one way of understanding this development, see, for instance, Bruno Latour, *Reassembling the Social: An Introduction to Actor-Network-Theory* (Oxford: Oxford University Press, 2005) and Bruno Latour, ed., *Reset Modernity!* (Karlsruhe: ZKM & Cambridge, MA: MIT Press, 2016).

18. This is a notion that Wolfgang Ernst will address in *Delayed Presence*, a forthcoming contribution to The Contemporary Condition book series.

19. Julieta Aranda et al., "Editorial —'The End of the End of History?' Issue Two," *e-flux journal*, no. 57 (2014), accessed August 22, 2016, http://www.e-flux.com/journal/editorial-the-end-of-the-end-of-history-issue-two/.

20. Giorgio Agamben, *Infancy and History: On the Destruction of Experience*, trans. Liz Heron (London: Verso, 1993 [1978]), 99.

Our overall hypothesis is thus that contemporaneity—understood with Osborne as the coming together of different, but equally "present" temporalities or "times"—is a decisive element of the globalization of our historical present. We propose to investigate this contemporaneity, this temporality of globality itself, with closer attention to the ways in which informational and computational technologies have helped, and still help, to make it possible.[21] One compelling way of conceptualizing this issue can be found in the work of sociologist and architectural theorist Benjamin Bratton, according to whom smart grids, cloud computing, mobile software and smart cities, universal addressing systems, ubiquitous computing and robotics are not unrelated genres of computation but constitute a larger and coherent whole, an "accidental megastructure" in the form of a planetary-scale computational system, which he names "The Stack":

> Planetary-scale computation takes different forms at different scales: energy grids and mineral sourcing; chthonic cloud infrastructure; urban software and public service privatization; massive universal addressing systems; interfaces drawn by the augmentation of the hand, of the eye, or dissolved into objects; users both overdetermined by self-quantification and exploded by the arrival of legions of nonhuman users (sensors, cars, robots). Instead of seeing the various species of contemporary computational technologies as so many different genres of machines, spinning out on their own, we should instead see them as forming the body of an accidental megastructure. Perhaps these parts align,

21. In stressing contemporaneity to be a *condition*, we refer to Jean-François Lyotard's *La condition postmoderne. Rapport sur le savoir* (Paris: Minuit, 1979) that also argued that teleological notions of human history were untenable largely as a consequence of developments in communications technology and computer science.

layer by layer, into something not unlike a vast (if also incomplete), pervasive (if also irregular) software and hardware *Stack*.[22]

Marking the interconnection of all these multiple layers and the interpenetration between digital and analogue times, and computational, material and human times, Bratton's conceptualization may be seen as a neat way of visualizing the information architectures and infrastructures that enables contemporaneity and the coming together of times. A critical point for us therefore is that technical, social, human and nonhuman layers are folded together to produce new forms of subjectivation at multiple scales through such means. This is what cultural theorist and activist Tiziana Terranova has called an "infrastructure of autonomization" that limits our operational and imaginative potential.[23] She is making reference to Marx's views on automation, particularly in his "Fragment on Machines," as a description of how machines subsume the knowledge and skill of workers into wider assemblages.[24] Subjects are now produced in relation to these interlocking computational infrastructures in which other agents such as algorithms generalize massive amounts of data, and furthermore "machine learning" techniques produce corresponding forms of knowledge bound to hegemonic systems of power and prejudice. The increasing use of relational machines such as search engines is an example of

22. Benjamin H. Bratton, "The Black Stack," *e-flux journal*, no. 53 (2014), accessed August 24, 2016, http://www.e-flux.com/journal/the-black-stack/#_ftn1. See also his recently published *The Stack: On Software and Sovereignty* (Cambridge, MA: MIT Press, 2016).

23. Tiziana Terranova, "Red Stack Attack! Algorithms, Capital and the Automation of the Common," *Effimera* (2014), accessed August 24, 2016, http://effimera.org/red-stack-attack-algorithms-capital-and-the-automation-of-the-common-di-tiziana-terranova/.

24. Automation is described by Marx as a process of absorption in the machine of the "general productive forces of the social brain" (also referred to elsewhere as "general intellect"), in "Fragment on Machines," in *Grundrisse: Foundations of the Critique of Political Economy (Rough Draft)*, trans. Martin Nicolaus (Harmondsworth: Penguin, 1981), 705–706. See also Franco Berardi, *The Soul at Work: From Alienation to Autonomy* (Cambridge, MA: MIT Press, 2009).

the ways in which knowledge is filtered at the expense of the specific content or detail on how it was produced. There is also a sense in which the world begins to be produced through the logic of predictive modelling—following the cultural logic of "premediation"[25]—and correspondingly it changes what people do and how they behave based on what is imagined will happen in the future: "The more effectively the models operate in the world, the more they tend to normalize the situations in which they are entangled. This normalization can work in very different ways, but it nearly always will stem from the ways in which differences have been measured and approximated within the model."[26] The autonomization serves to demonstrate how the various computational layers "intermingle" as a real-time system within further systems to provide a dynamic model of the emergent infrastructures that operate upon us as new forms of sovereignty and governance.[27] But they also offer new possibilities for what technological cultures scholar Adrian Mackenzie more optimistically identifies as "trans-individual cooperative potential."[28] (We return to the issue of trans-individuation later.)

How time is managed and manipulated by informational machines is clearly an important component of how different experiences of time are brought together and how they are compressed, and it seems evident that our experiences are more and more aligned to their temporal operations. The computer is temporal in its internal structure and attention

25. We use Richard Grusin's term to indicate how future events are "pre-mediated" before they happen, in *Premediated: Affect and Mediality after 9/11* (Basingstoke: Palgrave Macmillan, 2010).

26. Adrian Mackenzie, "The Production of Prediction: What Does Machine Learning Want?," *European Journal of Cultural Studies* 18, no. 4–5 (2015): 442.

27. This description is close to what Antoinette Rouvroy calls "algorithmic governmentality." See, for instance, her "Technology, Virtuality and Utopia: Governmentality in an Age of Autonomic Computing," in *The Philosophy of Law Meets the Philosophy of Technology: Computing and Transformations of Human Agency*, eds. Mireille Hildebrandt and Antoinette Rouvroy (London: Routledge, 2011), 136–157.

28. Adrian Mackenzie, "The Production of Prediction: What Does Machine Learning Want?," 443.

to computational processes can reveal epistemic aspects otherwise largely overlooked in cultural analysis. The concept of "micro-temporality," associated with the media archaeology of Wolfgang Ernst, offers one useful way to develop a "time-critical" analysis of events taking place within technical systems and an alternative way of analyzing and conceptualizing the way they function and somewhat determine our experience and behaviors.[29] It seems to us that we need to develop a techno-materialist understanding of what is happening at various temporal scales, and across layers of machine operations through detailed technical description, in order to analyze and better understand contemporaneity. In our endeavour to develop a suitable vocabulary that better reflects contemporary conditions, we find the scalar notion of the Stack—itself a technical term to indicate how data is exchanged and stored sequentially—potentially useful as it has the epistemological precision of a technical concept while also working in a cultural register.

In the light of these comments we might also examine the evocative phrase "real-time" as it appears to encapsulate the contemporary condition. Put simply, real-time refers to the effect of information being delivered seemingly as it happens, reflecting the demand for ever-faster transactions and instantaneous feedback across global networks. In computing, it serves to describe the computer processing time—the actual time elapsed in the performance of a computation by a computer—in which the operation appears to be immediate and able to correspond instantaneously to an external process, as for example, with the fluctuations of financial markets that operate at the level of micro- or nanoseconds. Nevertheless real-time is not real but mediated, it stands for a human rather than a machine sense of time and is only ever an approximation

29. Wolfgang Ernst, *Digital Memory and the Archive*, ed. Jussi Parikka (Minneapolis: University of Minnesota Press, 2013).

(or the endless deferral of real time) as there is always a degree of delay in the system in which it operates. The term "near real-time" is a more accurate description and often used to highlight the deferral between the occurrence of an event and the use of the processed data, indicated by the buffering effects when streaming audio or video data from the internet. It is the machine that is crucial in producing our experience of real-time that is only ever happening nearly at the same time as the event even if the difference seems more and more indistinguishable. We include these considerations because the experience of "real-time" (not to mention the way the notion has entered our everyday language) and thus of co-presence—or rather pseudo-co-presence—through digital communication technologies is a decisive factor in the coming into being of contemporaneity and testifies to a change in our experience of time (and space) itself.

When does something begin and end within such dynamic technical operations? A stream of data produces differences due to the outside influence of things that are executing and running in real-time, making the stream decidedly unpredictable, temporal and rhythmic. In our enforced confusion, we are captivated by the apparent simplicity of the graphical spinning wheel icon of a "throbber" that indicates when a computer program is performing an action such as downloading content or performing intensive calculations.[30]

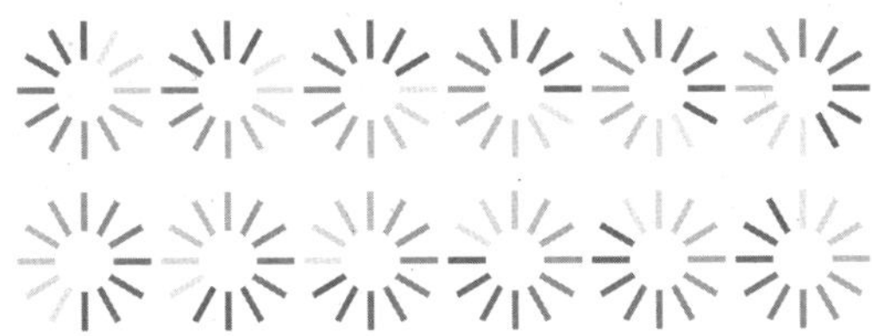

30. See the wikipedia entry on Throbber, https://en.wikipedia.org/wiki/Throbber. Also see Winnie Soon, "At the time of execution: throbber.start()," paper for *.exe (ver0.1) (2015), accessed August 24, 2016, http://softwarestudies.projects.cavi.au.dk/index.php/Exe0.1_Winnie_Soon.

In contrast to the teleology of a progress bar, a throbber does not convey how much of the action has been completed and resonates with our understanding of the real-time dynamics of the contemporary condition and the ambiguity of the temporal registers that are running seemingly at the same time.[31]

* * *

Our scope for this essay is wide and our approach unashamedly eclectic. Approaching the question, phenomenon, idea, or fiction even, of contemporaneity seems to force us into bringing together different epistemological registers that are not usually brought into dialogue and that do not easily communicate with each other. It is, however, our belief that it is necessary to break the confines of these registers and disciplines in order to grasp contemporaneity and its possible consequences. This is because contemporaneity cannot be limited to a certain feeling or relation to time, to a historical period, to a particular development in technology, to a phase of capitalism, to whatever is present at the same time, and so on. It has a number of different dimensions and aspects to it, which are not mutually exclusive. In our endeavor not to merely consider contemporaneity as a matter of fact, but rather turn it into a matter of concern (to borrow a formulation from Bruno Latour),[32] it may seem to some readers that we are drawing together too many competing discourses and epistemological registers. But it seems to us that this kind of messy interdisciplinary inquiry is perfectly suited to its object of study that already draws from divergent spatial and temporal axes. The concept of contemporaneity refers to

31. For these reasons we have adopted this icon for our research project The Contemporary Condition as seen on the reverse cover of this book and on our webpage, http://www.contemporaneity.au.dk.

32. Bruno Latour, "From Realpolitik to Dingpolitik, or How to Make Things Public," in *Making Things Public: Atmospheres of Democracy*, ed. Bruno Latour and Peter Weibel (Cambridge. MA: MIT Press, 2005), 4–31.

temporal complexity on many different scales, ranging from the individual to the collective, from the local and microcosmic to the global and the planetary. We would therefore argue for a transversal approach that aims to embrace the ways that different lines of enquiry intersect in topological structures that suggest recombinatory possibilities and reappropriations of space and time.[33] This may or not be good scholarship but more to the point it allows for a coming together of concepts and ideas that break from traditional hierarchizations and conceptual paradigms and instead introduces inventive forms of assembling meaning that oscillate between the registers of the human subject, media, and culture. Together these registers form a transversal framework for establishing intersections of different lines of inquiry and methodologies that we utilize in this essay—and more fully in the book series of which it is a part—to open up a further diversity of perspectives, including a more planetary one which necessitates a slowing down and deepening of time.[34] The point however is not to agree to any kind of settlement of these axes but to recognize that they converge and diverge and as such produce dynamic tensions and slippages of meaning.

To date there has been little systematic research on the very phenomenon of contemporaneity and its consequences. As we have indicated through our outline above we consider there to be three broad lines of inquiry that require further work. Firstly, existing research on "contemporary art" focuses mainly—very roughly put—on three different qualities when defining the character of contemporary art, namely the media used, the subject matter, and/or the historical moment

33. This is broadly the conceptual premise of the online journal *transversal*, http://eipcp.net/transversal. On transversality, see Gilles Deleuze, *Foucault* (New York: Continuum, 1999).

34. See, for instance, other books released as part of our book series: Terry Smith's *The Contemporary Composition*, The Contemporary Condition 02 (Berlin: Sternberg Press, 2016) and Jussi Parikka's *A Slow, Contemporary Violence: Damaged Environments of Technological Culture*, The Contemporary Condition 03 (Berlin: Sternberg Press, 2016).

of its making public. Across decisive differences we see the tendency to focus on media evident in, for instance, art and media theorist Boris Groys' understanding of installation as the medium of contemporary art and art historian and critic Rosalind E. Krauss' frustration with "the post-medium condition."[35] The more content-oriented understanding of what constitutes contemporary art might be seen in curator and writer Nicolas Bourriaud's relational aesthetics, in art historian and critic Claire Bishop's detection of a social turn, or in curator and writer Charles Esche's modest proposals;[36] whereas the understanding of contemporary art as relating to "the present time" is a more common sense notion of the contemporary. In making a distinction from existing research on the notion of "contemporary art"—and notwithstanding finding the analyses mentioned useful—we focus on the issue of temporality, on the added complexity of temporality that the concept of contemporaneity stands for.

Secondly, the more nuanced research on contemporary art, especially in the work of Osborne and Smith, explicitly relates contemporary art to the issue of contemporaneity.[37] These perspectives stress the complexity of today's cultural formations mainly through bringing contemporary art history and theory in dialogue with philosophy of time, philosophy of

35. See Boris Groys, "The Topology of Contemporary Art," in *Antinomies of Art and Culture: Modernity, Postmodernity, Contemporaneity*, ed. Terry Smith et al. (Durham: Duke University Press, 2008), 71–80; Rosalind E. Krauss, *A Voyage on the North Sea: Art in the Age of the Post-Medium Condition* (London: Thames & Hudson, 2000); Krauss, *Perpetual Inventory* (Cambridge, MA: MIT Press, 2010); and Krauss, *Under Blue Cup* (Cambridge, MA: MIT Press, 2011).

36. See Claire Bishop, *Radical Museology: or, What's 'Contemporary' in Museums of Contemporary Art?* (London: Koenig Books, 2013); Claire Bishop, *Artificial Hells: Participatory Art and the Politics of Spectatorship* (London: Verso, 2012); Nicolas Bourriaud, *L'esthétique rélationelle* (Dijon: Les presses du réel, 1998); Nicolas Bourriaud, *The Radicant* (New York: Lukas & Sternberg, 2009); and Charles Esche, *Modest Proposals* (Istanbul: Baglam Press, 2005).

37. On this question, in addition to Osborne and Smith, see Hans Belting, *The End of the History of Art*, trans. Christopher S. Wood (Chicago: University of Chicago Press, 1987 [1983]); Arthur C. Danto, *After the End of Art: Contemporary Art and the Pale of History* (Princeton: Princeton University Press, 1998); and Keith Moxey, *Visual Time: The Image in History* (Durham: Duke University Press, 2013).

history, and historical analysis. We would like to extend this existing research on contemporaneity and contemporary art by investigating the significant role of media and information technology in the production and the representation of contemporaneity. We suggest to stress the technological aspect through close attention to media and computational processes as well as to the ways in which contemporary artistic practices thematize and investigate the extreme spatial and temporal compression occasioned by networked architectures such as the Internet. The work of contemporary artist and writer Hito Steyerl, for example, can be said to speculate on the impact of the Internet and digitization on the fabric of our everyday lives and our experience of time.[38] Her work articulates and reflects upon the global circulation of images, the "iconomy," and the workings of computational realities and how digital culture and network relations, rather than those of place, increasingly mediate social relations and the social imaginary.

A way to conceive of contemporary art that departs from a traditional formalistic focus on medium and post-medium might also be seen in art historian and critic David Joselit's idea of "after art." In the book of the same name he analyses the power and potency of images and argues for a critical contemporary art "after art." He regards the image explosion of our current globalized—and digitized—society of the spectacle as a *condition* of contemporary art (and architecture) and shifts focus from the production and exhibition of art works to the life and circulation of works outside the closed context of art. This is a shift from discrete individual objects and unique works to their effects in the networks of circulating images that are working, or at work, in the world. Thus, Joselit argues for shifting critical attention from the *production* of art

38. See Nick Aikens, ed., *Too Much World: The Films of Hito Steyerl* (Van Abbemuseum, Eindhoven & Berlin: Sternberg Press, 2014).

to what images *do* when they circulate and enter into diverse networks—seeing aesthetic objects as forms crystallizing out of a population of images. According to Joselit contemporary art exists as a fold or disruption within a *population* of images, or what he—employing a technical vocabulary, and partly inspired by Latour's notion of "assemblage"—calls a "format" understood as a pattern of links or connections: "Our real work begins *after art*, in the networks it formats."[39] He furthermore develops a concept of "the aggregrator," which "makes hyper-accumulation eloquent by causing asynchronous objects to occupy a common space [...] making the unevenness of globalization plastic and visible."[40] We find these concepts of the format and the aggregator useful in trying to develop a vocabulary to analyze and come to terms with the phenomenon of contemporaneity in relation to contemporary art.[41]

As well as time can no longer be conceived as blank and homogeneous, media and their mediality—the ways in which media function as such—can no longer be conceived as neutral and transparent processes, subordinate to the informational content they convey. Rather, they possess a social and cultural agency. Actually, it is—according to the post-phenomenological thinking of philosopher of technology Bernard Stiegler—through technology and media that our very consciousness of time is established to begin with.[42] As we learn from Heidegger's analysis, the fundamental human experience

39. David Joselit, *After Art* (Princeton: Princeton University Press, 2013), 96.

40. David Joselit, "On Aggregators," *October*, no. 146 (Fall 2013): 18.

41. It should be noted, however, that Joselit has reservations about Osborne's definition of contemporaneity as "the coming together of different, but equally 'present' temporalities or 'times' in our historical present." In a discussion with Jacob Lund at the conference "Aesthetics, Contemporaneity, Art," at Aarhus Institute for Advanced Studies, May 28–30, 2015, he stated that such a condition of contemporaneity is nothing historically new as this was also the case in for instance London of the nineteenth century. We claim that the interconnection of times at a planetary scale, even though it is uneven, is indeed historically new as it cannot any longer be confined to particular, localizable centers. See also Joselit, "On Aggregators," 10, for a critique of Osborne's understanding of contemporary art as postconceptual art.

42. Bernard Stiegler, *La technique et le temps* I–III (Paris: Éditions Galilée, 1994–2001).

of the temporal can be understood in terms of an original *ek-stasis*, which transgresses an interior subjecthood and connects the individual to its surroundings. The temporal comes into being through a constant movement of exteriorization and interiorization. Today it becomes increasingly evident that this continuous process of exteriorization of our consciousness—and the necessarily concomitant constant interiorization of the surroundings toward which it reaches out—is dependent upon media and information technologies in the form of computers, tablets, and smart phones; that our surroundings to a larger and larger extent is constituted by these technologies.

We follow this premise that technics and technical objects determine our experience of time as they facilitate access to the past and anticipation of the future, that is, individual as well as collective memory and *ekstacy* (or retention and protention as Stiegler,[43] based on Husserl, would have it). Put simply, our relation to time is constituted or "mediated" by the technical means through which it is apprehended. Thus, our conception of contemporaneity builds upon an understanding of media not merely as a means of communication and as narrowly technical entities, but also as environments within which forms of life are developed. For us, the important term "trans-individuation," developed in the work of Gilbert Simondon and Stiegler in particular, describes this co-development or co-individuation of the individual "I," the collective "we," and the media and technologies through which they communicate, exteriorize and subjectify themselves. The constantly increasing integration of information technologies in our everyday lives occasion changes in our sensorium and in order to analyze these it is necessary to further develop our concept of media and mediality. This ecological interest in media—which can be traced back to Marshall McLuhan—could for instance be

43. See Bernard Stiegler, "Memory" (with an introduction by Mark B. N. Hansen), in *Critical Terms for Media Studies*, ed. W. J. T. Mitchell and B. N. Hansen (Chicago: University of Chicago Press, 2010): 66–87.

seen in the exhibition "New Sensorium: Exiting from Failures of Modernization," shown at ZKM in Karlsruhe in 2016. In the accompanying brochure the curator Yuko Hasegawa interestingly stresses the focus of the participating artists on investigating the interdependency and pre-connectivity within such environments:

> The artists in this exhibition discover, select, and invent potential media (intermediary tools of communication) or mediality, in a much larger, comprehensive context that includes physicality, emotions, and relationships with the surrounding environment. Here, the term mediality is not based on the idea of "mediation," where exchange happens between two communicating agents, or "inter-action," where things act upon one another. Rather, mediality is grasped to be discussed on the premise of media ecologies where everything is pre-connected, and that "intra-actions" (a neologism introduced by Karen Barad) occur from within subjects and objects comprising that ecology.[44]

Thus, apart from the global connectedness via different media and information technologies and our general immersion within these—which makes it impossible to comprehend human interaction and subject formation independently of surrounding media—an investigation of mediality in contemporary art should not least be motivated by the development within the object of study. Very broadly speaking, artistic practice can be claimed to have moved from a modernist medial self-interrogation, to a postmodernist so-called "post-medial" installation art, to—in dialogue with technological development, especially within digital media—a resumption of the question of mediality and its influence on the process of meaning-making

44. Yoko Hasegawa, "New Sensorium. Exiting from Failures of Modernization," in *New Sensorium. Exiting from Failures of Modernization*, exhibition brochure, ed. ZKM (Karlsruhe: ZKM, 2016), 11.

and issues such as subjectivity and memory. Based on the work of, among others, Simondon, Stiegler, and Jacques Rancière, we consider media to be dynamical entities, as environments or places-in-between for meaning-making and symbolic exchange where processes of individuation and subjectivation take place.[45] It is through such environments that different times and different experiences of time come together in a shared present, which, when regarded at a macro-level where also the Stack is in operation, can be understood as what historian Harry Harootunian calls a "thickly-filled temporality" with multiple, commingling pasts and thus as constituting a unity of uneven temporalizations differentiating global geopolitical space.[46]

Yet it is also important to develop a time-critical analysis that uses methods where media—and not just humans—become epistemologically active and allow us to perceive what is knowable or even unknowable. The "forensic materiality" of Matthew Kirschenbaum and the "micro-temporality" of Ernst, for instance, provide ways to suspend human-centeredness (at least temporarily) and focus attention on the deep material structures of machines and their potential epistemological insights.[47]

45. See Gilbert Simondon, *L'individuation psychique et collective* (Paris: Aubier, 1989); Bernard Stiegler, *De la misère symbolique* I–II (Paris: Éditions Galilée, 2004–05); Jacques Rancière, *Le partage du sensible: Esthétique et politique* (Paris: Fabrique, 2000); Jacques Rancière, "What Medium can Mean," *Parrhesia*, no. 11 (2011): 35–43; and Jacob Lund, "Artistic Re-Appropriation and Reconfiguration of the Medium's Milieu," in *The Nordic Journal of Aesthetics*, no. 44–45 (2012–13): 109–28.

46. See Harry Harootunian, "Uneven Temporalities/Untimely Pasts: Hayden White and the Question of Temporal Form," in *Philosophy of History After Hayden White*, ed. Robert Doran (London: Bloomsbury, 2013): 119–149.

47. Matthew G. Kirschenbaum, *Mechanisms: New Media and the Forensic Imagination* (Cambridge, MA: MIT Press, 2008); Ernst, *Digital Memory and the Archive*. In connection to this, we might also draw attention to the work of the Forensic Architecture research agency based at Goldsmiths, University of London (http://www.forensic-architecture.org) and Eyal Weizman's notion of "Forensic Temporality," in *Simulation, Exercise, Operations*, ed. Robin Mackay (2015), accessed August 24, 2016, https://www.urbanomic.com/chapter/simulation-exercise-operations-forensic-temporality/; as well as Knut Ebeling's development of a material conception of time in *Wilde Archäologien 2. Theorien der Materialität der Zeit von Archiv bis Zerstörung* (Berlin: Kadmos Kulturverlag, 2016) and "The Art of Searching: On 'Wild Archaeologies' from Kant to Kittler," *The Nordic Journal of Aesthetics*, no. 51 (2016, forthcoming).

Shifting attention from the discursive to the nondiscursive realm, Ernst would go as far as to suggest that technological machine time challenges historicist notions of progressive continuity and technical repeatability executes "an almost ahistorical functional reenactment."[48] By this he means that media archaeological reenactments operate more directly than the narrative form of history and thus are able to reveal new forms of knowledge on the level of their actual appearance. To Ernst these are time-machines, and although recording technologies are historical in a general sense, in terms of their technical and discursive context the mechanism itself is able to "operate as an island of non-historical eventual-ity," as he puts it.[49] What unfolds, within the operations of algorithms too, is a reordering of time itself that no longer can be considered to develop in a particular order or through a sequence of actions, thus leaving analysis subject to those same conditions.

In addition to how computation begins to undo some of our assumptions about how and what knowledge is produced, alongside the critique of the anthropocentrism of Western thinking, we might also briefly mention other points of slippage or instability of epistemic authority related to the ways in which space and time are understood. Of particular interest to us here is the work of philosopher and feminist theorist Karen Barad. Drawing on the work of the physicist Niels Bohr, she refers to how the "entanglements" of matter and meaning account for various other confusions and contingencies that make strict definitions between past and future distinctly unreliable.[50] In saying that states, events, and processes are constantly renegotiated without recourse to any pre-existing notion of space and time, she is referring to both Heisenberg's "uncertainty principle" that confirms the trade-off between

48. Ernst, *Digital Memory and the Archive*, 175.

49. Ernst, *Digital Memory and the Archive*, 182.

50. Karen Barad, *Meeting the Universe Halfway: Quantum Physics and the Entanglement of Matter and Meaning* (Durham: Duke University Press, 2007).

knowing more or less about position and momentum, and to Bohr's "complementarity principle" as a means to understand how individual things have complementary properties which cannot be observed or measured at all at the same time. Bohr's epistemological framework is employed to establish how an object is not independent of its scientific observation but is part of a set of conditions under which knowledge is produced in a wider network of discursive and nondiscursive relations.

In short, we support Barad's endeavor to challenge the "epistemological and ontological inseparability of the apparatus from the objects and the subjects it helps to produce; and produces new understandings of materiality, discursivity, agency, causality, space, and time."[51] It follows that there is not only the realization that there are uncertainties over space and time but also the realization that apparatuses do not simply change in time but materialize through time (what she calls a "mutated time-space regime"). Temporality under these conditions becomes a more open process, less deterministic, or straightforwardly causal in activating the movement from cause to effect, more performative and open ended in the production of meanings. The way we think about spaces and times are made more open to other possibilities of critical political practice where indeterminacy, contingency, and ambiguity coexist with causality and determinacy (and thus even previously opposing positions can be brought together). The conceptual framework of this essay hopefully begins to make more sense with this qualification not least in the ways we oscillate between what might seem to be awkwardly competing technical and cultural registers.

If the investigation of the issue of temporality is the first distinguishing mark of our approach to contemporaneity and attention to the active role of technology the second, we would thirdly argue that most existing research on contemporary

51. Barad, *Meeting the Universe Halfway*, 200.

art and culture neglects artistic practice itself as a means to provide epistemic inquiry. Here we also follow the assumption that contemporary art can operate as an advanced laboratory for investigating processes of meaning-making and for understanding wider developments within culture and society. Our approach thus pays close attention to contemporary artistic and curatorial practices as forms of research—with a particular interest in the role of contemporary technologies —not only as analytical material but more as modes of investigative practice which can make epistemic claims in and of themselves. We end this essay with an example of how this works in practice by reflecting on the design of this book as a way of accessing an imaginary that we believe is not simply delimited by the contemporary condition.

The book series of which this one is an integral part attempts to address contemporaneity in terms of its distinct technological form using more dynamic conceptions of mediality and materiality as outlined in this essay. In this way we hope it is apparent that information technologies contribute to uncertainties over space and time and may open up a more indeterminate, contingent and ambiguous space for thinking and action. This takes place across spaces and temporalities and also at different scales that draw together the various elements that are also very present in the material-discursive practices of writing and publishing. As authors we are presented with the difficulty of expressing our thoughts on a complex topic and unfolding a processual argument in a book, which is in itself a temporal object in danger of undoing our argument through its teleological form. As we write we are also aware that the resulting text occupies different temporalities of writing and reading, and that the real-time collaborative writing environment we are using to write with is subject to its own particularities of distributed and synchronous production (not to mention ownership). On the one hand we aim to draw attention to this through serialization—a book series—and how the books we produce can be read together and apart (as it should be stressed that we aim this book to operate both in its own right and as an introduction to the series). We also are aware of working under conditions that allow our writing to become more evidently like programming inasmuch as it begins to produce a reflexive form that includes its textual form and the technology that inscribes it.[52]

The art/design work of Dexter Sinister provides an example of how practice contributes to our thinking and writing in this respect. Each book uses a bespoke version of their typeface "Meta-The-Difference-Between-The-Two-Font," itself based on MetaFont developed by the computer scientist Donald Knuth in the late 1970s.[53] MTDBT2F is both a description language that defines the actual font and its own interpreter that executes its final form, and thus encourages readers to consider the contributing role of technology in the production of meaning and their experience of reading. Dexter Sinister themselves elaborate on this in a brief note on the type that repeats on the last page of each book in the series.[54]

It is our assumption that it is fruitful to investigate the accelerated role of media and information technologies at multiple scales in relation to our core concerns of subjectivity, mediation, and culture in this way, focusing on how contemporaneity and its consequences are represented and

52. Moreover we might draw attention to the performing arts form of Live Coding where programmers edit the code while it is running. See http://toplap.org/. Coding practices express an imaginary based on the ability to shape and predict a future based on the manipulation and reanimation of past data. On the politics and aesthetics of coding, see Geoff Cox, *Speaking Code: Coding as Aesthetic and Political Expression* (Cambridge, MA.: MIT Press, 2013).

53. Details on Knuth's Metafont can be found at https://en.wikipedia.org/wiki/Metafont.

54. Dexter Sinister have also written extensively about the project and its history in *Bulletins of The Serving Library*. See "A Note on the Type," http://www.servinglibrary.org/journal/1/a-note-on-the-type and "Letter & Spirit," http://www.servinglibrary.org/journal/3/letter-and-spirit, as well as the related essay "A Note on the Time," http://www.servinglibrary.org/journal/1/a-note-on-the-time.

```
** initialization complete. **\r
Welcome to Meta-the-Difference-Between-the-Two-Font.
Today is Fri Mar  2 15:27:30 EST 2012
*
Current working directory is /Users/reinfurt/Documents/Projects/META THE DIFFERE
NCE BETWEEN THE 2 FONT/Source/Meta-the-difference between-the-two-Font/v0.6c
```

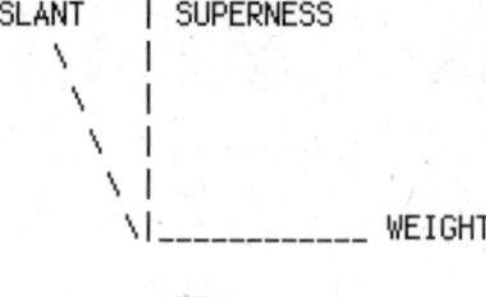


```
                         PEN ===>

WEIGHT=50.00000000000000000000
SLANT=.20000000000000000000
SUPER=.57500000000000000000
PENTYPE=0
PENX=349.50000000000000000000
PENY=100
PENR=216.00000000000000000000
Welcome to Meta-the-Difference-Between-the-Two-Font.
Today is Fri Mar  2 15:27:30 EST 2012
*
Current working directory is /Users/reinfurt/Documents/Projects/META THE DIFFERE
NCE BETWEEN THE 2 FONT/Source/Meta-the-difference between-the-two-Font/v0.6c
mftrace 1.2.16
Font `mtdbt2f4d'...
Using encoding file: `/usr/local/texlive/2011basic/texmf/fonts/enc/dvips/tetex/m
tdbt2f.enc'
Running Metafont...
Tracing bitmaps... [0][1][2][3][4][5][6][7][8][9][10][11][12][13][14][15][16][17
][18][19][20][21][22][23][24][25][26][27][28][29][30][31][32][33][34][35][36][37
][38][39][40][41][42][43][44][45][46][47][48][49][50][51][52][53][54][55][56][57
][58][59][60][61][62][63][64][65][66][67][68][69][70][71][72][73][74][75][76][77
][78][79][80][81][82][83][84][85][86][87][88][89][90][91][92][93][94][95][96][97
][98][99][100][101][102][103][104][105][106][107][108][109][110][111][112][113][
114][115][116][117][118][119][120][121][122][123][124][125][126][127][129][130][
131][132][134][135][136][137][138][140][141][142][143]
Assembling raw font to `mtdbt2f4d.pfa.raw'...
Copyright (c) 2000-2011 by George Williams.
 Executable based on sources from 13:48 GMT 22-Feb-2011-D.
 Library based on sources from 13:48 GMT 22-Feb-2011.
** metafont ok **
** fontforge ok **
** mtdbt2f ok **
Bye.
** mtdbt2f-make ok **
Bye.
** sleep for 0 seconds **
```

Output log for Dexter Sinister's Meta-The-Difference-Between-The-Two-Font while the script is running and generating a new font. Used with permission.

experienced through, and as, art. Furthermore it seems necessary to develop a more dynamical concept of the very media and technologies that enable contemporaneity where these are seen as constituting broader environments for meaning-making and symbolic exchange.[55] Following the work of Simondon, Stiegler, and Félix Guattari we regard them as dynamical entities where all members — including nonhuman — participate in the environment and are functions of it, where processes of contemporary identity and subject formation take place, and where our social imaginary comes into being.[56] If we seem to have lost our ability to conceive of history as a transformative force in society, we would like to stress the importance of the need to rethink the deep structures of temporalization that render our present the way it is in order to create possibilities for imagining it differently.

55. See Jacob Lund, "Artistic Re-Appropriation and Reconfiguration of the Medium's Milieu," for an elaboration of the understanding of media as environments or *mi-lieux*.

56. See Félix Guattari, *Les trois écologies* (Paris: Éditions Galilée, 1989) and references to Simondon and Stiegler above.

BIBLIOGRAPHY

Agamben, Giorgio. *Infancy and History: On the Destruction of Experience* [1978]. Translated by Liz Heron. London: Verso, 1993.
——. "What is the Contemporary?" [2008]. In *What is an Apparatus? And Other Essays*, 39–54. Translated by David Kishik and Stefan Pedatella. Stanford: Stanford University Press, 2009.

Aikens, Nick, ed. *Too Much World: The Films of Hito Steyerl.* Van Abbemuseum, Eindhoven & Berlin: Sternberg Press, 2014.

Alberro, Alexander. "Periodising Contemporary Art." In *Theory in Contemporary Art Since 1985.* Edited by Zoya Kocur and Simon Leung, 64–71. Malden, MA: Wiley-Blackwell, 2012.

Aranda, Julieta et al. "Editorial–'The End of the End of History?' Issue Two," *e-flux journal,* no. 57 (September 2014). Accessed August 24, 2016. http://www.e-flux.com/journal/editorial-the-end-of-the-end-of-history-issue-two/.

Augé, Marc. *Pour une anthropologie des mondes contemporains.* Paris: Aubier, 1994.

Barad, Karen. *Meeting the Universe Halfway: Quantum Physics and the Entanglement of Matter and Meaning.* Durham, NC: Duke University Press, 2007.

Belting, Hans. *The End of the History of Art.* Translated by Christopher S. Wood. Chicago: University of Chicago Press, 1987 [1983].

Benjamin, Walter. "On the Concept of History." In *Selected Writings, vol. 4, 1938–1940.* Edited by Howard Eiland and Michael W. Jennings, 389–400. Cambridge, MA: Belknap Press, 1992.

Berardi, Franco. *The Soul at Work: From Alienation to Autonomy.* Cambridge, MA: MIT Press, 2009.

Bishop, Claire. *Artificial Hells: Participatory Art and the Politics of Spectatorship.* London: Verso, 2012.
——. *Radical Museology: or, What's 'Contemporary' in Museums of Contemporary Art?,* London: Koenig Books, 2013.

Bourriaud, Nicolas. *L'esthétique relationelle.* Dijon: Les presses du réel, 1998.
——. *The Radicant.* New York: Lukas & Sternberg, 2009.

Bratton, Benjamin H. “The Black Stack.” *e-flux journal*, no. 53 (2014). Accessed August 24, 2016. http://www.e-flux.com/journal/the-black-stack/#__ftn1.
——. *The Stack: On Software and Sovereignty*. Cambridge, MA: MIT Press, 2016.

Chakrabarty, Dipesh. *Provincializing Europe: Postcolonial Thought and Historical Difference*. Princeton NJ: Princeton University Press, 2000.

Cox, Geoff. “Postscript on the Post-Digital and the Problem of Temporality.” In *Postdigital Aesthetics: Art, Computation and Design*. Edited by David M. Berry and Michael Dieter, 151–162. Basingstoke: Palgrave Macmillan, 2015.

Cox, Geoff, and Alex McLean. *Speaking Code: Coding as Aesthetic and Political Expression*. Cambridge, MA: MIT Press, 2013.

Cox, Geoff, and Jacob Lund. “Contemporary Conditions are Badly Known.” *Acoustic Space*, 2017, forthcoming.

Cox, Geoff, Nicolas Malevé, Michael Murtaugh. “Archiving the Data-body: Human and Nonhuman Agency in the Documents of Kurenniemi.” In *Writing and Unwriting Media Art History*. Edited by Jussi Parikka and Joasia Krysa, 125–142. Cambridge, MA: MIT Press, 2015.

Danto, Arthur C. *After the End of Art: Contemporary Art and the Pale of History*. Princeton: Princeton University Press, 1998.

Deleuze, Gilles. *Foucault*. New York: Continuum, 1999.

Dexter Sinister. *Bulletins of The Serving Library*. Accessed August 24, 2016. http://www.servinglibrary.org/journal.

Didi-Huberman, Georges. *L'Œil de l'histoire*, I–IV. Paris: Minuit, 2009–12.

Ebeling, Knut. *Wilde Archäologien 2. Theorien der Materialität der Zeit von Archiv bis Zerstörung*. Berlin: Kadmos Kulturverlag, 2016.
——. “The Art of Searching: On ‘Wild Archaeologies’ from Kant to Kittler.” *The Nordic Journal of Aesthetics*, no. 51 (2016, forthcoming).

Ernst, Wolfgang. *Das Rumoren der Archive. Ordnung aus Unordnung*. Berlin: Merve Verlag, 2002.

——. "Media Archaeography: Method and Machine versus History and Narrative of Media." In *Media Archaeology: Approaches, Applications and Implications*. Edited by Erkki Hutamo and Jussi Parikka, 239–255. Berkeley: University of California Press, 2011.
——. *Digital Memory and the Archive*. Edited by Jussi Parikka. Minneapolis: University of Minnesota Press, 2013.
——. "The Archive as Metaphor. From Archival Space to Archival Time." In *Open* #7 (2005). Accessed August 24, 2016. http://archivepublic.wordpress.com/texts/wolfgang-ernst/.
——. *Delayed Presence*. The Contemporary Condition 04. Berlin: Sternberg Press, 2017 (forthcoming).

Esche, Charles. *Modest Proposals*. Istanbul: Baglam Press, 2005.

Fukuyama, Francis. *The End of History and the Last Man*. Los Angeles: Avon Books, 1992.

Groys, Boris. "The Topology of Contemporary Art." In *Antinomies of Art and Culture: Modernity, Postmodernity, Contemporaneity*. Edited by Terry Smith, Okwui Enwezor, and Nancy Condee, 71–80. Durham: Duke University Press, 2008.

Grusin, Richard. *Premediation: Affect and Mediality after 9/11*. Basingstoke: Palgrave Macmillan, 2010.

Guattari, Félix. *Les trois* écologies. Paris: Galilée, 1989.

Harootunian, Harry. "Remembering the Historical Present." *Critical Inquiry*, vol. 33, no. 3 (Spring 2007): 471–494.
——. "Uneven Temporalities/Untimely Pasts: Hayden White and the Question of Temporal Form." In *Philosophy of History After Hayden White*. Edited by Robert Doran, 119–49. London & New York: Bloomsbury, 2013.

Hartog, François. *Régimes d'historicité: Présentisme et expériences du temps*. Paris: Seuil, 2003.

Harvey, David. *The Condition of Postmodernity*. Oxford: Basil Blackwell, 1989.

Hasegawa, Yuko. "New Sensorium. Exiting from Failures of Modernization." In *New Sensorium. Exiting from Failures of Modernization*, exhibition brochure. Edited by ZKM, 10–14. Karlsruhe: ZKM, 2016.

Heidegger, Martin. *Sein und Zeit*. Tübingen: Niemeyer, 1986 [1927].
——. *Being and Time*. Translated by J. Stambaugh. Albany: SUNY Press, 2010.

Jameson, Fredric. *A Singular Modernity: Essay on the Ontology of the Present*. London: Verso, 2002.
——. *Archaeologies of the Future. The Desire Called Utopia and other Science Fictions*. London: Verso, 2005.

Joselit, David. *After Art*. Princeton: Princeton University Press, 2013.
——. "On Aggregators." *October*, no. 146 (Fall 2013): 3–18.

Kirschenbaum, Matthew G. *Mechanisms: New Media and the Forensic Imagination*. Cambridge, MA: MIT Press, 2008.

Koselleck, Reinhart. *Vergangene Zukunft: Zur Semantik geschichtlicher Zeiten*. Frankfurt am Main: Suhrkamp, 1979.
——. *Zeitschichten: Studien zur Historik. Mit einem Beitrag von Hans-Georg Gadamer*. Frankfurt am Main; Suhrkamp, 2000.

Krauss, Rosalind E. *A Voyage on the North Sea: Art in the Age of the Post-Medium Condition*. London: Thames & Hudson, 2000.
——. *Perpetual Inventory*. Cambridge, MA: MIT Press, 2010.
——. *Under Blue Cup*. Cambridge, MA: MIT Press, 2011.

Latour, Bruno. "From Realpolitik to Dingpolitik, or How to Make Things Public." In *Making Things Public: Atmospheres of Democracy*. Edited by Bruno Latour and Peter Weibel, 4–31. Cambridge, MA: MIT Press, 2005.
——. *Reassembling the Social: An Introduction to Actor-Network-Theory*. Oxford: Oxford University Press, 2005.
——. ed. *Reset Modernity!* Karlsruhe: ZKM & Cambridge, MA: MIT Press, 2016.

Lund, Jacob. "Artistic Re-appropriation and Reconfiguration of the Medium's *Milieu*." *The Nordic Journal of Aesthetics* no. 44–45 (2012–13): 109–128.
——. "Acts of Remembering in the work of Esther Shalev-Gerz: From Embodied to Mediated Memory." In *Why Now and How?: Holocaust Mediation in the Post-Witness Era*. Edited by Diana Popescu and Tanja Schult, 28–43. London: Palgrave Macmillan, 2015.
——. "The Coming Together of Times: Jean-Luc Godard's Aesthetics of Contemporaneity and the Remembering of the Holocaust." *The Nordic Journal of Aesthetics*, no. 49–50 (2015): 138–155.

——. “Destroying the Image in Order to Save It: Contemporary Image-Politics in the Work of Alfredo Jaar.” In *Kreative Zerstörung: Über Macht und Ohnmacht des Destruktiven in den Künsten.* Edited by Wolfram Bergande. Vienna: Turia & Kant, 2016 (forthcoming).

Lyotard, Jean-François. *La condition postmoderne. Rapport sur le savoir.* Paris: Minuit, 1979.

Mackenzie, Adrian. “The Production of Prediction: What Does Machine Learning Want?” *European Journal of Cultural Studies* 18, no. 4–5 (2015): 442.

Marx, Karl. *Grundrisse: Foundations of the Critique of Political Economy (Rough Draft).* Translated by Martin Nicolaus. Harmondsworth: Penguin, 1981.

Mbembe, Achille. *On the Postcolony.* Berkeley: University of California Press, 2001.

McLuhan, Marshall, and Quentin Fiore. *The Medium is the Massage: An Inventory of Effects.* New York: Bantam, 1967.

Moxey, Keith. *Visual Time: The Image in History.* Durham: Duke University Press, 2013.

Nora, Pierre. “L’avènement mondial de la mèmoire.” *Transit* no. 22 (2002), 18–31, accessed August 24, 2016, http://www.eurozine.com/articles/article__2002-04-19-nora-fr.html.

Osborne, Peter. *The Politics of Time: Modernity and Avant-Garde.* London: Verso, 1995.
——. “Temporalization as Transcendental Aesthetics: Avant-Garde, Modern, Contemporary.” *The Nordic Journal of Aesthetics*, no. 44–45 (2012–13): 28–49.
——. *Anywhere or not at all: Philosophy of Contemporary Art.* London: Verso, 2013.
——. “Existential Urgency: Contemporaneity, Biennials and Social Form.” *The Nordic Journal of Aesthetics*, no. 49–50 (2015): 175–188.

Papastergiadis, Nikos. *Cosmopolitanism and Culture.* Cambridge: Polity, 2012.

Papastergiadis, Nikos, and Victoria Lynn, eds. *Art in the Global Present.* Sydney: UTS ePress, 2014, accessed August 22, 2016, http://epress.lib.uts.edu.au/books/art-global-present.

Parikka, Jussi. *A Slow, Contemporary Violence: Damaged Environments of Technological Culture*, The Contemporary Condition 03. Berlin: Sternberg Press, 2016.

Rancière, Jacques. *Le partage du sensible: Esthétique et politique.* Paris: Fabrique, 2000.
——. *Malaise dans l'esthétique.* Paris: Galilée, 2004.
——. "What Medium can Mean." *Parrhesia*, no. 11 (2011): 35–43.
Rouvroy, Antoinette. "Technology, Virtuality and Utopia: Governmentality in an Age of Autonomic Computing." In *The Philosophy of Law Meets the Philosophy of Technology: Autonomic Computing and Transformations of Human Agency.* Edited by Mireille Hildebrandt and Antoinette Rouvroy, 136–157. London: Routledge, 2011.

Ruin, Hans. "Time as Ek-stasis and Trace of the Other." In *Rethinking Time: Essays on History, Memory, and Representation.* Edited by Hans Ruin and Andrus Ers, 51–62. Stockholm: Södertörn Philosophical Studies 10, 2011.

Simondon, Gilbert. *L'individuation psychique et collective.* Paris: Aubier, 1989.

Smith, Terry. "Contemporary Art and Contemporaneity." *Critical Inquiry*, vol. 32, no. 4 (Summer 2006): 681–707.
——. *What is Contemporary Art?* Chicago: University of Chicago Press, 2009.
——. *Contemporary Art: World Currents.* London: Laurence King Publishing, 2011.
——. *Thinking Contemporary Curating.* New York: Independent Curators International, 2012.
——. "Contemporary Art: World Currents in Transition Beyond Globalization." In *The Global Contemporary: The Rise of New Art Worlds after 1989.* Edited by Hans Belting, Andrea Buddensieg, and Peter Weibel, 186–192. Cambridge, MA: MIT Press for ZKM, Karlsruhe, 2013.
——. *The Contemporary Composition.* The Contemporary Condition 02. Berlin: Sternberg Press, 2016.

Smith, Terry, Okwui Enwezor, and Nancy Condee, eds. *Antinomies of Art and Culture: Modernity, Postmodernity, Contemporaneity.* Durham: Duke University Press, 2008.

Soon, Winnie. "At the time of execution: throbber.start()." Paper for *.exe (ver0.1) (2015). Accessed August 24, 2016. http://softwarestudies.projects.cavi.au.dk/index.php/Exe0.1__Winnie__Soon.

Steyerl, Hito. “Too Much World: Is the Internet Dead?” *e-flux journal*, no. 49 (November 2013). Accessed August 24, 2016. http://www.e-flux.com/journal/too-much-world-is-the-internet-dead/.

Stiegler, Bernard. *La technique et le temps* I–III. Paris: Éditions Galilée, 1994–2001.
——. Stiegler, Bernard. *De la misère symbolique* I–II. Paris: Éditions Galilée, 2004–05.
——. “Memory” (with an introduction by Mark B. N. Hansen). In *Critical Terms for Media Studies*. Edited by W. J. T. Mitchell and Mark Hansen, 66–87. Chicago: University of Chicago Press, 2010.

Terranova, Tiziana. “Red Stack Attack! Algorithms, Capital and the Automation of the Common.” *Effimera* (2014). Accessed August 24, 2016. http://effimera.org/red-stack-attack-algorithms-capital-and-the-automation-of-the-common-di-tiziana-terranova/.

Weizman, Eyal. “Forensic Temporality.” In *Simulation, Exercise, Operations*. Edited by Robin Mackay (2015). Accessed August 24, 2016. https://www.urbanomic.com/chapter/simulation-exercise-operations-forensic-temporality/.

Geoff Cox is Associate Professor in the School of Communication and Culture, Aarhus University (DK), and also adjunct faculty at Transart Institute (DE/US). He is co-editor of the online open access academic journal *APRJA* (with transmediale), published (with Alex McLean) *Speaking Code* (MIT Press 2013), and is currently working on a multi-authored book on live coding.

Jacob Lund is Associate Professor of Aesthetics and Culture and Director of the research programme Mediality, Materiality, Aesthetic Meaning in the School of Communication and Culture at Aarhus University. Amongst other things, he is Editor-in-Chief of *The Nordic Journal of Aesthetics*.

Together they are engaged on the 3 year research project The Contemporary Condition, funded by the Danish Council for Independent Research (contemporaneity.au.dk).

PEN = 0,1,1,0, WEIGHT = 25, SLANT = 0, SUPERNESS = 0.71

The typeface used to set this series is called Meta-The-Difference-Between-The-Two-Font (MTDBT2F), designed by Dexter Sinister in 2010 after MetaFont, a digital typography system originally programmed by computer scientist Donald Kunth in 1979.

Unlike more common digital outline fonts formats such as TrueType or Postscript, a MetaFont is constructed of strokes drawn with set-width pens. Instead of describing each of the individual shapes that make up a family of related characters, a MetaFont file describes only the basic pen path or *skeleton* letter. Perhaps better imagined as the ghost that comes in advance of a particular letterform, a MetaFont character is defined only by a set of equations. It is then possible to tweak various parameters such as weight, slant, and superness (more or less bold, Italic, and a form of chutzpah) in order to generate endless variations on the same bare bones.

Meta-The-Difference-Between-The-Two-Font is essentially the same as MetaFont, abiding the obvious fact that it swallows its predecessor. Although the result may look the same, it clearly can't be, because in addition to the software, the new version embeds its own backstory. In this sense, MTDBT2F is not only a tool to generate countless PostScript fonts, but *at least equally* a tool to think about and around MetaFont. Mathematician Douglas Hofstadter once noted that one of the best things MetaFont might do is inspire readers to chase after the intelligence of an alphabet, and "yield new insights into the elusive 'spirits' that flit about so tantalizingly behind those lovely shapes we call 'letters.'"

For instance, each volume in The Contemporary Condition is set in a new MTDBT2F, generated at the time of publication, which is to say *now.*

Dexter Sinister, 23/09/16, 09:54 AM